Ketogenic Desserts & Snacks

38 Delicious Low Carb Fat Burning Recipes

Table Of Contents

Chapter Three: 6 Ketogenic Cake Recipes

Chapter Four: 6 Ketogenic Dessert Bars

Ketogenic Lemon Bars

Ketogenic Coconut Nut Bars

Ketogenic Blondies with Pumpkin

Ketogenic Fudge Peanut Butter Bars

Ketogenic Chocolate Brownies

Ketogenic Candy Bars

Chapter Five: 6 Ketogenic Ice Cream Recipes

Holiday Ice Cream

Thanksgiving Pumpkin Ice Cream

Ketogenic Strawberry Ice Cream

Salty Butterscotch Ice Cream

Peanut Butter Chocolate Ice Cream

Ketogenic Coffee Ice Cream

Chapter Six: 10 Other Ketogenic Dessert Recipes

Ketogenic Maple Nut Muffins

Ketogenic Lemon Scones

Ketogenic Pumpkin Donut Holes

Ketogenic Pink Lemonade Mousse

Ketogenic Peanut Butter Chocolate Fudge

Ketogenic Peanut Almond Butter Balls

Ketogenic Raspberry Popsicles

Ketogenic Peanut Butter Bombs

Ketogenic Coconut Yogurt

Chocolate Covered Bacon

Tips to Help When Keto Cooking

Conclusion

☐

Introduction

If you have purchased this book, then it is likely that you are looking for recipes to spice up and keep your ketogenic diet interesting. The fact is, that while the ketogenic diet works wonders for weight loss as well as for controlling a number of health concerns, it can be hard to follow when you have a sweet tooth!

With so many recipe books out there for the ketogenic diet, many that are noticeably absent are those that address delicious keto friendly desserts and snacks. That is precisely how this book came to be. As someone with enjoys those tasty bites and who understands the benefits of keto dieting, I had to find a way to keep things in check. I needed to find a way to control those cravings without ruining a day's progress. Most of all, however, I had to find easy recipes that didn't taste like I'd just taken a mouth full of protein powder.

At first, I began making just about every keto friendly dessert and snack recipe I could find. I made them all, kept recipes in binders, and tweaked ingredients until I was sure I got things right. Only then did I decide to pull together my own book of recipes, a book of touched up, refined desserts and snacks that were worth spending time in the kitchen for.

So, if you're like me and have been hunting for a way to make keto with a sweet tooth more bearable, then read on!

Chapter One: A Brief Ketogenic Overview

In this chapter, I will help you to:

- Review the basics of the ketogenic diet

- Know what is important to ketogenic eating

- Know what to avoid when eating keto

Reviewing the Ketogenic Diet

The chances are, that if you are reading this book and looking for ketogenic friendly recipes, then you already have an idea of what keto eating means. Lets's take a brief moment to recap the very basics.

When we consume food rich in carboydrates the body then converts these into glucose. Glucose is the most easily accessible source of energy and the body turns to it first to fuel its basic functions. When glucose is used, fat is not, and so that fat is then stored in the body. The excess fat then inevitably leads to weight gain.

Once of the most significant sources of glucose in our diet is the breakdown of carbohydrates. So, it makes sense that if we reduce our carbohydrate consumption, we give our bodies less glucose to use as fuel and simply force it to break down fat for fuel instead. This reduction in carbohydrate consumption puts the body in to a state called ketosis.

Ketosis is a natural process in which the body responds to a lowered intake of carbohydrates by breaking down fat stored in the liver. This breakdown of fats results in ketones being released, hence the term ketosis.

Therefore, when we eat a ketogenic diet, the aim is to put our body in to the natural process of ketosis. To do this, we eat higher fat content and lower carb content.

What to Remember When Cooking Keto

When cooking on a ketogenic diet it is important to remember that you are aiming for low carbohydrate and high fat content. You need to be aware of more than just your carbohydrate gram level, but also your fiber and sugar content.

Your fiber content is important because it is used to calculate your net carbs. It is your net carbohydrate level that you are focusing on keeping track of when eating keto. This is simply calculated by subtracting the fiber grams from the carbohydrate grams.

Your sugar content is important because sugars are carbohydrates. Generally speaking, high carbohydrate foods are high in sugars, so you should always monitor your sugar intake. In the recipes that follow there is a full nutritional guide to keep you on track.

What to Avoid When Eating Keto

In addition to general carbohydrates and sugars, when eating deserts and snacks on the ketogenic diet you need to be particularly watchful of certain food types including:

- Spices with high carbohydrate levels

- Fruit juices

- Excess sugary fruits

- Diet soda, processed foods

- Foods high in MSG

- Grains

- Refined oil and fats, trans fats

- Alcohol

- Overuse of artificial sweeteners

Chapter Two: 10 Ketogenic Cookie Recipes

In this chapter, you will learn how to make the following delicious ketogenic cookie recipes:

- Ketogenic Chocolate Coconut Cookies

- Ketogenic Nut Butter Cookies

- Ketogenic Strawberry Thumbprint Cookies

- Ketogenic Coconut Macaroon Cookies

- Ketogenic Pumpkin Spice Cookies

- Ketogenic Chocolate Chip Cookies

- Ketogenic Peanut Butter Chocolate Cookies

- Ketogenic Snickerdoodle Cookies

- Ketogenic Coffee Time Cookies

- Ketogenic Peanut Butter Cookies

- ## *Ketogenic Chocolate Coconut Cookies*

Servings:	20
Nutrition Per Serving	
Calories:	77
Fat:	6.8g
Protein:	2.2g
Carbs:	2.5g
Sugar:	0g
Fiber:	1.5g

Ingredients

- 1 cup almond flour

- 2 eggs (unchilled)

- ½ tsp. baking powder

- 1/3 cup unsweetened shredded coconut

- ¼ cup cocoa powder

- ¼ cup coconut oil

- 3 tbsp. coconut flour

- 1/3 cup erythritol

- ¼ tsp. salt

- 1 tsp. vanilla extract

Directions:

1. Preheat your oven to 350 degrees. While your oven preheats, line a large cookie sheet with parchment paper.

2. In a medium sized mixing bowl, combine your dry ingredients and mix well using your hand mixer.

3. In a separate bowl, combine all of your wet ingredients together and mix well using your hand mixer.

4. Slowly add your wet ingredient mixture to your dry ingredient mixture while mixing until all of your ingredients are combined.

5. Now, break off small pieces of your dough and roll them in to small cookie balls. You should be able to get around 20 balls out of your bowl of dough. Set each of your cookie balls on to your parchment covered sheet.

6. Bake your cookies in your preheated oven for 15 to 20 minutes or until cooked through.

• *Ketogenic Nut Butter Cookies*

Servings:	10
Nutrition Per Serving	
Calories:	235
Fat:	22g
Protein:	5g
Carbs:	11g
Sugar:	1g
Fiber:	4g

Ingredients

- 1 egg

- 8.8 oz. almond butter

- ¼ tsp. salted butter

- ¼ cup powdered erythritol

- ¼ cup raw coconut butter

Directions:

1. Preheat your oven to 320 degrees. While your oven preheats, cover a large cookie sheet with parchment paper.

2. Melt your almond butter in a double boiler or in a bowl inside a saucepan of hot water.

3. Once your almond butter has melted remove your bowl from the pan and take the pan off your heat. Now, add in your salt, erythritol, and egg to the bowl of melted almond butter.

4. With a silicone spatula, fold your ingredients together until fully mixed together.

5. Once your ingredients are well mixed, break your dough in to 10 pieces. Roll each piece between your hands to make balls of dough. Set each ball of dough on to your parchment paper covered cookie tray.

6. Gently flatten your cookies using the palm of your hand or a fork.

7. Bake your cookies for 12 minutes in your preheated oven until browned.

• *Ketogenic Strawberry Thumbprint Cookies*

Servings:	16
Nutrition Per Serving	
Calories:	95
Fat:	9g
Protein:	2g
Carbs:	4g
Sugar:	0g
Fiber:	3g

Ingredients

- 2 tbsp. coconut flour

- 1 cup almond flour

- ½ tsp. baking powder

- 1 tbsp. shredded coconut

- 2 tbsp. sugar-free strawberry jam

- 2 eggs

- 4 tbsp. coconut oil

- ½ cup Erythritol

- ½ tsp. salt

- ¼ tsp. cinnamon

- ½ tsp. almond extract

- ½ tsp. vanilla extract

Directions:

1. Preheat your oven to 350 degrees. While your oven preheats, cover a large cookie sheet with parchment paper.

2. In a large mixing bowl use a whisk to mix together all of your dry ingredients. Once well mixed, make a well in the center of your dry ingredients and add in your wet ingredients. Use your whisk again to combine the dry and wet ingredients together.

3. If necessary, use your hands to finish mixing your dough. Once well mixed, break your dough in to 16 pieces and roll each one in to a ball.

4. Set your balls of dough on the parchment covered cookie sheet and use your thumb to press a thumbprint in the center of each cookie.

5. Bake your cookies in the preheated oven for 15 minutes or until golden but not overdone. Set your cookies out on a cookie rack to cool completely.

6. Once your cookies are cooled, add a small amount of your strawberry jam in to each thumbprint and sprinkle with your coconut.

- ## *Ketogenic Coconut Macaroon Cookies*

Servings:	12
Nutrition Per Serving	
Calories:	88
Fat:	8g
Protein:	1g
Carbs:	4g
Sugar:	1g
Fiber:	2g

Ingredients

- 1 cup unsweetened shredded coconut

- 1 egg white

- 1 dash salt

- 2 tbsp. coconut oil

- ¼ cup erythritol

- ½ tsp. almond extract

Directions:

1. Preheat your oven to 350 degrees. While your oven preheats, cover a large cookie sheet with parchment paper.

2. Spread your coconut out on to the parchment covered cookie sheet. When your oven comes to heat, toast the coconut until browned. Once browned, take your coconut out of the oven and let it cool completely.

3. Now in a large mixing bowl, use a hand mixer to beat your egg white until it doubles in size and add your salt and erythritol as you are still mixing.

4. Pour in your almond extract and your toasted cooled coconut and mix together thoroughly.

5. Use your hands to roll 12 balls out of your dough and lay them out on your parchment covered cookie sheet.

6. Bake your macaroons for around 15 minutes or until golden brown.

- ## *Ketogenic Pumpkin Spice Cookies*

Servings:	15
Nutrition Per Serving	
Calories:	75
Fat:	7g
Protein:	2g
Carbs:	3g
Sugar:	1g
Fiber:	2g

Ingredients

- 1 ½ cup almond flour

- ½ tsp. baking powder

- 1 egg

- ½ cup pumpkin puree

- ¼ cup salted butter

- 1 tsp. vanilla extract

- ¼ cup erythritol

- 25 drops liquid Stevia

- 2 extra drops of erythritol

- 1 tsp. pumpkin pie spice

Directions:

1. Preheat your oven to 350 degrees. While your oven preheats, cover a large cookie sheet with parchment paper.

2. In a large mixing bowl, combine your baking powder, flour, and ¼ cup erythritol. Stir together with a silicone spatula.

3. In a clean microwave safe bowl, combine your pumpkin puree, butter, vanilla, and liquid Stevia. Microwave the mixture for a few seconds to soften the ingredients up (don't melt your butter!)

4. Add in your microwaved ingredients in to your dry ingredients. Mix well using your silicone spatula until you get a sticky dough.

5. Use a teaspoon to scoop your dough in to 15 servings and use your hands to roll each serving in to a ball. Set

the cookie balls on to your parchment paper and use your palm to flatten each one gently.

6. Put your cookies in the oven to bake for 12 minutes.

7. As your cookies bake, add your 2 drops of erythritol to your pumpkin pie spice and use your food processor to mix together.

8. When your cookies have cooked through, sprinkle the top of each with your pumpkin pie spice mixture out of the food processor.

- ## *Ketogenic Chocolate Chip Cookies*

Servings:	16
Nutrition Per Serving	
Calories:	162
Fat:	12g
Protein:	3g
Carbs:	13g
Sugar:	6g
Fiber:	3g

Ingredients

- 1 cup almond flour

- 2 tbsp. coconut flour

- ½ tsp. baking powder

- 2 tbsp. psyllium husk powder

- 3 tbsp. whey protein

- 1 egg

- 1 cup dark chocolate chips

- 8 tbsp. room temperature unsalted butter

- ¼ cup erythritol

- 2 tsp. vanilla extract

- 10 drops liquid Stevia

Directions:

1. Preheat your oven to 350 degrees. While your oven preheats, cover a large cookie sheet in parchment paper.

2. In a large mixing bowl, combine your coconut flour, almond flour, baking powder, psyllium husk powder, and whey protein. Stir with a silicone spatula to combine your ingredients.

3. Now, in a clean medium sized mixing bowl, use your hand mixer to mix the butter for just a couple of minutes until it pales. Add in 10 drops of your liquid Stevia and ¼ cup of erythritol and mix again to combine.

4. Add your vanilla extract and egg in to the butter bowl and mix again until you get a smooth batter.

5. Once your butter is smooth, use a sieve to sift your dry ingredients over the butter ingredients. Use your hand mixer again to combine your ingredients fully.

6. Set your hand mixer down and use your spatula to fold in your dark chocolate chips evenly. Once your chocolate chips are folded in, pull off small pieces of dough and roll them in to cookie balls. You should get 16 cookies.

7. When your cookie balls are laid out on your cookie sheet, use your palm or the bottom of a drinking glass to flatten your cookies gently.

8. Bake your cookies for between 12 and 15 minutes until done.

• *Ketogenic Peanut Butter Chocolate Cookies*

Servings:	20
Nutrition Per Serving	
Calories:	262
Fat:	23g
Protein:	3g
Carbs:	15g
Sugar:	7g
Fiber:	5g

Ingredients

- 2 ½ cups almond flour

- 1 ½ tsp. baking soda

- 1 ½ tsp. baking powder

- ½ tsp. salt

- 3 tbsp. no sugar added maple syrup

- ½ cup natural creamy peanut butter

- 20 Hershey's dark chocolate minis

- 1 tbsp. vanilla extract

- ¼ cup coconut oil

- ¼ cup erythritol

Directions:

1. In a large mixing bowl, combine ¼ cup coconut oil, ½ cup peanut butter, 1 tbsp. vanilla extract, and 3 tbsp. maple syrup. Use your hand mixer to mix these ingredients together until you get a smooth batter.

2. In a second mixing bowl, combine 1 ½ tsp. baking powder, 2 ½ cups almond flour, ½ tsp. salt, and ¼ cup erythritol. Stir these ingredients together with a silicone spatula to combine.

3. Once well mixed, use a sieve to sprinkle your dry ingredients over your batter. Use your mixer to combine all of the ingredients in your bowl until you get a gritty dough.

4. Now, use your hands to roll the dough in to a big round ball and wrap it tightly in a sheet of plastic wrap. Put your wrapped dough in the refrigerator and let sit for 30 minutes.

5. Preheat your oven to 350 degrees while your dough chills.

6. Unwrap your 20 mini dark chocolate pieces and then cover a large cookie sheet with parchment paper.

7. When your dough is chilled, take it out of the oven and divide it in to 20 pieces. Wrap each piece of dough around a single dark chocolate mini piece. Make sure that the chocolate is completely surrounded by dough when folding your cookies.

8. Bake your cookies for 15 minutes or until completely cooked and allow to cool before eating.

- ## *Ketogenic Snickerdoodles*

Servings:	14
Nutrition Per Serving	
Calories:	132
Fat:	12.4g
Protein:	3.4g
Carbs:	4.2g
Sugar:	5.5g
Fiber:	2.2g

Ingredients

- 2 cups almond flour

- ¼ tsp. baking soda

- ¼ cup maple syrup

- ¼ cup coconut oil

- 1 tbsp. vanilla

- 7 drops liquid Stevia

- Dash of salt

- 2 tbsp. cinnamon

- 2 tbsp. erythritol

Directions:

1. Preheat your oven to 350 degrees. While your oven preheats, cover a large cookie sheet with parchment paper.

2. In a large mixing bowl, combine 1 tbsp. vanilla, ¼ cup melted coconut oil, 7 drops liquid Stevia, and ¼ cup maple syrup. Use a silicone spatula to stir your ingredients together.

3. In another bowl, combine ¼ tsp. baking soda, a dash of salt, and 2 cups almond flour. Mix together well and then slowly add in your wet ingredients to your dry. Mix thoroughly until you get a cookie dough.

4. Now, use a small bowl to combine your 2 tbsp. erythritol and 2 tbsp. cinnamon. Mix these together.

5. Use your hands to roll your cookie dough in to 14 small balls and roll each ball in your cinnamon mixture to cover it completely.

6. Set out your covered cookie balls on your parchment covered cookie sheet and use the palm of your hand of the bottom of a glass to flatten them gently.

7. Bake your cookies for 10 minutes and then pull them out of the oven to cool.

- ## *Ketogenic Coffee Time Cookies*

Servings:	10
Nutrition Per Serving	
Calories:	167
Fat:	17.1g
Protein:	3.9g
Carbs:	2.8g
Sugar:	7.4g
Fiber:	1.4g

Ingredients

- 1 ½ cups almond flour

- ½ tsp. baking soda

- ½ tsp. salt

- ½ cup room temperature unsalted butter

- 1 tbsp. and 1 tsp. instant coffee grounds

- 2 eggs

- 1/3 cup erythritol

- 17 drops liquid Stevia

- 1 ½ tsp. vanilla extract

- ¼ tsp. cinnamon

Directions:

1. Begin by preheating your oven to 350 degrees. While your oven preheats, cover a large cookie tray with parchment paper.

2. In a large mixing bowl, combine your 1 ½ cups almond flour, ½ tsp. baking soda, ½ tsp. salt, coffee grounds, and ¼ tsp. cinnamon. Stir with a silicone spatula to mix thoroughly.

3. Using two small bowls or short drinking glasses, crack your eggs, separating your whites and yolks.

4. Now, add your butter to a clean bowl and whip it to a creamy consistency using your hand mixer. Once it's finished whipping, add in 1/3 cup erythritol and whip again using your hand mixer. This time you want to whip until your butter turns almost white.

5. When your butter is almost white, add your egg yolks and mix again until combined. Once combined, add half

of your dry ingredients in to your butter mixture and whip.

6. When half your dry ingredients are thoroughly mixed in to your wet ones, add 17 drops of liquid Stevia and 1 ½ tsp. vanilla extract along with the rest of your dry ingredients and then mix again until well combined.

7. Clean your mixer and then use it to whip your egg whites until you have stiff peaks and then fold them in to your dough.

8. Tear your dough in to 10 pieces, roll in to cookies and set on your baking sheet. Press down gently to flatten and then bake in your preheated oven for 12 minutes or until browned.

Ketogenic Peanut Butter Cookies

Servings:	18
Nutrition Per Serving	
Calories:	97
Fat:	8.5g
Protein:	2.4g
Carbs:	3.08g
Sugar:	4.3g
Fiber:	1.6g

Ingredients

- 1/3 cup coconut flour

- ¼ cup flaxseed meal

- 1 tbsp. heavy whipping cream

- ½ cup natural peanut butter

- 1/3 cup erythritol

- 1 tsp. baking powder

- ¼ tsp. baking soda

- 5 tbsp. salted butter

- 1 egg

Directions:

1. Preheat your oven to 350 degrees. While your oven preheats, cover a large cookie sheet with parchment paper.

2. In a large mixing bowl, mix together your heavy cream, butter, and peanut butter until combined. Then combine your baking powder, baking soda, coconut flour, erythritol, and flax seed meal in to this mixture. Stir to disperse your ingredients.

3. Crack your egg in to your ingredients and mix thoroughly. Once mixed, take your dough and make 18 rounded cookie balls. Place them on your cookie sheet and press down gently.

4. Bake your cookies for 15 minutes until done.

Chapter Three: 6 Ketogenic Cake Recipes

In this chapter, you will learn how to make the following mouthwatering ketogenic cake recipes:

- Ketogenic Spice Cakes

- Ketogenic Swiss Roll Cake

- Ketogenic Lemon Sponge Cake

- Ketogenic Chocolate Swirl Cheesecake

- Ketogenic Mini Cheesecakes

- Ketogenic Lime Cake with Blueberries

- # *Ketogenic Spice Cakes*

Servings:	12
Nutrition Per Serving	
Calories:	277
Fat:	27g
Protein:	6g
Carbs:	9g
Sugar:	1g
Fiber:	6g

Ingredients

- 2 cups almond flour

- 2 tsp. baking powder

- 4 eggs

- ½ cup salted butter

- 1 tsp. vanilla extract

- 5 tbsp. water

- ½ tsp. cinnamon

- ½ tsp. allspice

- ½ tsp. nutmeg

- ¼ tsp. ground clove

- ½ tsp. ginger

- ¾ cup erythritol

Directions:

1. Preheat your oven to 350 degrees. While your oven preheats, fill a cupcake tray with cupcake liners.

2. Now, in a large mixing bowl, combine ½ cup butter and ¾ cup erythritol. Use your hand mixer to mix them together until you get a smooth consistency.

3. Crack in two eggs and add your vanilla. Mix again with your hand mixer. Once smooth, add the rest of your eggs and mix again.

4. Once you have mixed in all four eggs, grind your clove down using a mortar and pestle. Once you get a fine powder, add it, along with all of your spices, to your bowl. Throw in your baking powder and mix well.

5. Add your almond flour in to your bowl and mix.

6. Add your water to the bowl and mix again.

7. Spoon your batter in to your cupcake liners and bake in your preheated oven for 15 minutes or until cooked through.

- ***Ketogenic Swiss Roll Cake***

Servings:	12
Nutrition Per Serving	
Calories:	391
Fat:	36g
Protein:	8g
Carbs:	24g
Sugar:	2g
Fiber:	15g

Ingredients

- 1 cup almond flour

- ¼ cup psyllium husk powder

- ¼ cup cocoa powder

- 1 tsp. baking powder

- 3 eggs

- ¼ cup coconut milk

- 4 tbsp. melted butter

- ¼ cup sour cream

- ¼ cup erythritol

- 1 tsp. vanilla

For Frosting:

- 8 oz. cream cheese

- ¼ cup sour cream

- 8 tbsp. butter

- 1 tsp. vanilla extract

- ¼ cup erythritol

- ¼ tsp. liquid Stevia

Directions:

1. Preheat your oven to 350 degrees. While your oven preheats, grease a baking pan.

2. In a mixing bowl, combine your cocoa powder, almond flour, psyllium husk powder, baking powder, and erythritol. Use a spatula to mix well.

3. In a small microwave safe bowl, melt 4 tbsp. butter in your microwave. Once melted, add this, 3 eggs, and ¼ cup sour cream in to your bowl of ingredients and mix together using a hand mixer.

4. Add 4 tbsp. coconut milk in to your bowl and continue to mix with your hand mixer.

5. On your greased baking sheet, spread out your batter. Bake this sheet of batter in your preheated oven for around 13 minutes or until set.

6. Once your cake has set, take it from the oven and set it aside to cool slightly.

7. Now, take a clean mixing bowl and combine 8 tbsp. butter, 8 oz. cream cheese, ¼ cup erythritol, ¼ cup sour cream, 1 tsp. vanilla extract, and ¼ tsp. liquid Stevia. Use your hand mixer to cream these filling ingredients together.

8. Once your filling is creamed, spoon it out on top of your cake sheet and spread it over the full top of the cake.

9. Gently roll up your cake sheet to trap the filling inside.

Ketogenic Lemon Sponge Cake

Servings:	6
Nutrition Per Serving	
Calories:	227
Fat:	20g
Protein:	9g
Carbs:	13g
Sugar:	1g
Fiber:	2g

Ingredients

- 1 cup almond flour

- 5 eggs

- ½ tsp. cream of tartar

- ¼ tsp. liquid Stevia

- ¼ tsp. salt

- 1 tsp. almond extract

- 1 tsp. baking powder

- 1 tsp. vanilla extract

- 1 tbsp. lemon zest

- ¼ cup erythritol

- 2 tbsp. olive oil

Directions:

1. Preheat your oven to 325 degrees. While your oven preheats, separate your eggs and grease a large cake pan, setting it on top of a cookie sheet.

2. In a medium sized mixing bowl, mix together your dry ingredients but leave out your cream of tartar.

3. In a fresh mixing bowl, mix together your 1 tsp. vanilla extract, ¼ tsp. liquid Stevia, egg yolks, and 1 tsp. almond extract using your hand mixer.

4. Now, add your dry ingredient mixture to your wet ingredient mixture using your hand mixer.

5. In a fresh mixing bowl, whip together ½ tsp. cream of tartar with your egg whites until you get peaks to your egg whites. Then add in your lemon zest and continue mixing until well incorporated.

6. Now, fold your egg whites gently in to the rest of your ingredients a little at a time. Once all of your ingredients are well combined, spoon them in to your cake pan.

7. Bake your cake for 25 minutes or until it is cooked through.

Ketogenic Chocolate Swirl Cheesecake

Servings:	16
Nutrition Per Serving	
Calories:	517
Fat:	42g
Protein:	9g
Carbs:	25g
Sugar:	16g
Fiber:	3g

Ingredients

- ¼ cup melted butter

- 24 oz. room temperature cream cheese

- 2 tbsp. low-carb baking mix

- 3 eggs separated

- 1 cup and 3 tbsp. Splenda

- 6 oz. melted sugar free dark chocolate

- 1 cup keto friendly cookie crumbs

- ½ cup chopped almonds

- 1 cup sour cream

Directions:

1. Preheat your oven to 350 degrees. While your oven preheats, grease a 9" cake pan.

2. In a medium sized mixing bowl, mix together your ½ cup almonds, butter, cookie crumbs, and 3 tbsp. Splenda. Mix together thoroughly and scrape in to the bottom of your cake pan. Press this mixture down to make a base crust and put the pan in to the refrigerator to chill.

3. Now, in another mixing bowl, use your hand mixer to stiffen your egg whites but keep them moist.

4. In yet another bowl, mix together your sour cream, flour substitute, 1 cup Splenda, and sour cream using your hand mixer. Once smooth, add your egg yolks gradually and continue to blend.

5. Once well mixed, fold your egg whites in to the bowl ingredients. Now, scoop your ingredients in to your cake pan over your chilled crust.

6. Add your melted chocolate to the top of the cake and swirl it using a knife to create a marble effect.

7. Set your cake pan on top of a cookie sheet and bake for 60 minutes or until cooked through. Allow your cake to cool and then chill in the refrigerator overnight.

- ## *Ketogenic Mini Cheesecakes*

Servings:	12
Nutrition Per Serving	
Calories:	269
Fat:	20g
Protein:	5g
Carbs:	14g
Sugar:	13g
Fiber:	1g

Ingredients

- ½ cup almond meal

- 16 oz. softened cream cheese

- ¼ cup melted butter

- 2 eggs

- 1 tsp. vanilla extract

- ¾ cup Splenda

Directions:

1. Preheat your oven to 350 degrees. While your oven preheats, fill a muffin pan with 12 paper liners.

2. In a medium sized mixing bowl, combine your butter and almond meal. Use a hand mixer to mix your ingredients together well and divide between your cupcake liners. Press your ingredients down in to the bottom of the cupcake liners.

3. In a clean bowl, combine your eggs, cream cheese, vanilla extract, and sweetener together. Mix together thoroughly before dividing over your cheesecake bases.

4. Bake your cakes in the oven for 15 minutes or until cooked through.

5. Once cooked, allow your cakes to cool and then refrigerate overnight to chill.

- ## *Ketogenic Lime Cake with Blueberries*

Servings:	10
Nutrition Per Serving	
Calories:	166
Fat:	14g
Protein:	6g
Carbs:	7g
Sugar:	2g
Fiber:	3g

Ingredients

- 1 cup almond flour

- 2 tbsp. coconut flour

- 2 tbsp. salted butter

- ¼ cup blueberries

- Zest 1 lime

- Juice 1 lime

- 5 eggs separated

- ¼ cup cream cheese

- 1 tsp. baking powder

- 2 tsp. blueberry extract

- ¼ tsp. liquid Stevia

- ¼ cup erythritol

Directions:

1. Preheat your oven to 325 degrees. While your oven preheats, grease two small loaf pans.

2. In a medium sized mixing bowl, combine all of your dry ingredients together and mix well with a silicone spatula.

3. In a clean mixing bowl, use your whisk to beat your egg yolks until they pale.

4. Now, add your blueberry extract, erythritol, liquid Stevia, cream cheese, and butter in to your egg yolks and continue to beat until you have a smooth consistency to your batter.

5. Next, add in your lime juice (but reserving 2 tsp.) and your lime zest and beat again to mix.

6. Use your sieve and sieve your dry ingredient mixture over your wet ingredients and mix well.

7. Now, add the reserved 2 tsp. of lime juice to your egg whites and beat with your hand mixer until you get stiff peaks. Then fold your egg whites in to your ingredients.

8. Use your silicone spatula to scoop your batter in to your loaf pans and then sprinkle your blueberries on top of the two loaves.

9. Bake your loaves for 35 minutes or until cooked through.

Chapter Four: 6 Ketogenic Dessert Bars

In this chapter, you will learn how to make the following tasty ketogenic dessert bars:

- Ketogenic Lemon Bars

- Ketogenic Coconut Nut Bars

- Ketogenic Blondies with Pumpkin

- Ketogenic Fudge Peanut Butter Bars

- Ketogenic Chocolate Brownies

- Ketogenic Candy Bars

- ## *Ketogenic Lemon Bars*

Servings:	16
Nutrition Per Serving	
Calories:	260
Fat:	19g
Protein:	5g
Carbs:	19g
Sugar:	12g
Fiber:	2g

Ingredients

- 2 cups almond flour

- 6 tbsp. butter

- 1 tbsp. fresh lemon zest

- 1/3 cup Splenda

For Your Filling

- 6 egg yolks

- ½ cup Splenda

- 2 tbsp. flavorless gelatin

- ½ cup butter

- ½ cup fresh lemon juice

- ¼ cup lemon zest

- ½ tsp. xanthan gum

Directions:

1. Begin by preheating your oven to 350 degrees. As your oven preheats, line an 8" x 8" square pan with parchment paper.

2. Now, in a small microwave safe dish, melt your 6tbsp. butter. Once melted, add your melted butter, 1/3 cup Splenda, 2 cups almond flour, and 1 tbsp. lemon zest to a medium sized mixing bowl. Stir well to combine thoroughly until you get a dough like consistency.

3. Once well mixed, press your dough in to the bottom of your square pan to make a crust. Put your crust in to the oven once preheated and bake for 10 minutes. Once baked, remove from the oven (leave the oven on for baking your filling) and set aside to cool completely while you make the filling.

4. Now, to make your filling, melt the rest of your butter in a small pan over low heat. Once your butter has melted completely, take your pan off the stove and use a whisk to mix in your lemon zest, Splenda, and lemon juice.

5. Once your ingredients have all dissolved in to your melted butter mixture, whisk in your egg yolks, then put your pan back on to the heat. Continue to whisk until your ingredients thicken in to a curd-like texture.

6. Once your mixture is thickened, take it off the stove and use a sieve to strain it in to a clean mixing bowl.

7. Use your whisk to whisk in your gelatin and xanthan gum. Keep whisking until your mixture is smooth and until everything has dissolved. Once this happens, pour your mixture over the baked crust.

8. Bake your filling covered crust in your preheated oven for 15 minutes. Once baked, remove your lemon bars from the oven and let them cool completely before cutting in to 16 pieces and serving.

Ketogenic Coconut Nut Bars

Servings:	8	
Nutrition Per Serving		
Calories:	124	
Fat:	10g	
Protein:	4g	
Carbs:	8g	
Sugar:	2g	
Fiber:	2g	

Ingredients

- 1 cup almond flour

- 1 dash salt

- ¼ cup melted butter

- ¼ cup sugar free maple syrup

- ¼ cup shredded coconut

- ½ cup cashews

- 1 tsp. cinnamon

Directions:

1. This is a no-bake bar, so there is no need to preheat your oven! You will need to line a 9" x 9" baking dish with parchment paper, however.

2. Now, take a medium sized mixing bowl and combine your almond flour and your melted butter. Use a silicone spatula to mix these ingredients together well.

3. Once mixed well, add in your maple syrup, cinnamon, and salt and continue to mix until well incorporated.

4. Now, mix in your shredded coconut.

5. Once your coconut is mixed in, chop up your cashews in to small pieces before mixing them in to your ingredients bowl. When everything is well mixed, mold it in to your baking dish. If desired, you can add more coconut or cinnamon on top of your bars.

6. Put your baking dish in to the refrigerator and let your bars chill completely for at least two hours before slicing in to 8 pieces to serve.

Ketogenic Blondies with Pumpkin

Servings:	12
Nutrition Per Serving	
Calories:	113
Fat:	11g
Protein:	2g
Carbs:	5g
Sugar:	1g
Fiber:	3g

Ingredients

- ¼ cup almond flour

- 2 tbsp. coconut flour

- 1 egg

- ½ cup pumpkin puree

- 1 oz. chopped pecans

- ½ cup room temperature butter

- 1 tsp. cinnamon

- 1/8 tsp. pumpkin pie spice

- 1 tsp. maple extract

- ½ cup erythritol

- 15 drops liquid Stevia

Directions:

1. Begin by preheating your oven to 350 degrees. While your oven preheats, grease a 9" x 9" baking pan or your favorite brownie pan.

2. Now, add your erythritol and your room temperature butter in a bowl and use your hand mixer to beat them together.

3. Once you have combined your erythritol and butter, add in your egg and continue to beat together your ingredients. Next, add in your Stevia, cinnamon, pumpkin pie spice, pumpkin puree, and maple extract. Mix thoroughly, before finally adding in your coconut flour and almond flour. Mix one last time.

4. With your ingredients well mixed, scoop them in to your greased pan. Sprinkle the top of your pan with your pecans.

5. Bake your blondies for 20 minutes or until set. Remove from the oven and allow them to cool completely before slicing in to 12 servings.

- ### *Ketogenic Fudge Peanut Butter Bars*

Servings:	8
Nutrition Per Serving	
Calories:	371
Fat:	34g
Protein:	7g
Carbs:	16g
Sugar:	2g
Fiber:	6g

Ingredients

Crust

- 1 cup almond flour

- 1 tbsp. erythritol

- ¼ cup melted butter

- Dash of salt

- ½ tsp. cinnamon

Fudge

- ½ cup natural smooth peanut butter

- ½ tsp. vanilla extract

- ¼ cup heavy cream

- ¼ cup melted butter

- 1/8 tsp. xanthan gum

- ¼ cup erythritol

Topping

- 1/3 cup chopped sugar-free dark chocolate

Directions:

1. Begin by preheating your oven to 400 degrees. While your oven preheats, cover the inside of a 9" x 9" baking dish with parchment paper.

2. Now we make the crust. Melt ½ cup of butter (the crust and fudge butter) in a microwave safe bowl.

3. Add ½ of your melted butter to a medium sized mixing bowl and pour in your crust cinnamon and crust

erythritol. Mix together your ingredients well and add in your dash of salt while mixing.

4. Once well mixed, press your bowl contents in to the bottom of your lined baking dish. Bake for 10 minutes in your oven until browned. Once browned, take it out of the oven and let it cool.

5. Now for the filling, pour all of your fudge ingredients in to a blender and blend together until thoroughly mixed.

6. When your filling ingredients are mixed completely, pour them over your cooled crust and spread evenly. Sprinkle the top with your broken dark chocolate pieces.

7. Put your baking pan in the refrigerator to chill completely overnight before cutting in to 8 pieces to serve.

- ## *Ketogenic Chocolate Brownies*

Servings:	8
Nutrition Per Serving	
Calories:	250
Fat:	23g
Protein:	9g
Carbs:	12g
Sugar:	1g
Fiber:	7g

Ingredients

- 2 cups almond flour

- 2 eggs

- ½ tsp. salt

- 1 tsp. baking powder

- ¼ cup sugar free low carb maple syrup

- ½ cup unsweetened cocoa powder

- ¼ cup coconut oil

- 1 tbsp. psyllium husk powder

- 2 tbsp. Torani salted caramel syrup

- 1/3 cup erythritol

Directions:

1. Preheat your oven to 350 degrees. While your oven preheats, grease an 11" x 7" baking dish or brownie pan.

2. Now, in a medium sized mixing bowl, add all of your wet ingredients together and beat together using a hand mixer.

3. Once your wet ingredients are well combined, add your dry ingredients in to a clean bowl and mix together well using a silicone spatula.

4. When your dry ingredients are mixed together well, add your wet ingredients in to your dry ingredients gradually while mixing.

5. Once all of your ingredients are well mixed together, pour them in to your greased baking dish or pan. Bake in the oven for 20 minutes until cooked through.

6. Once cooked through, take your brownies out of the oven and allow them to cool completely. Once cooled, cut in to 8 pieces and serve.

• *Ketogenic Candy Bars*

Servings:	16
Nutrition Per Serving	
Calories:	251
Fat:	23g
Protein:	9g
Carbs:	12g
Sugar:	1g
Fiber:	7g

Ingredients

Crust:

- 1 ¼ cup almond flour

- ¼ cup Stevia

- 15 drops liquid Stevia

- ¼ cup butter

- ½ tsp. xanthan gum

Filling:

- ½ cup natural creamy peanut butter

- ½ cup whipping cream

- ½ cup Stevia

- 1 tsp. vanilla extract

Topping

- 2 ½ oz. unsweetened chocolate

- 6 tbsp. butter

- 2 tbsp. cocoa powder

- 2 tbsp. Stevia

- 15 drops liquid Stevia

- ½ tsp. vanilla extract

Directions:

1. Begin by preheating your oven to 350 degrees. Now, grease an 8" x 8" baking dish.

2. Now, to make your crust, add your crust ingredients in to your blender and pulse until you get a crumbled texture.

3. Press your pulsed ingredients in to the bottom of your baking dish and then bake in your preheated oven for 15 minutes or until browned. Once browned, take it from the oven and set it aside to cool.

4. Next, to make your filling, put your Stevia in a small pot on the stove with 1 tsp. of water. Heat on medium-high heat while stirring until your water is bubbling and your Stevia is dissolved completely.

5. Take your pan off the heat and add in your cream. Continue stirring your mixture and put it back on the heat to allow it to come to a boil for 1 minute.

6. Remove your pan from the heat now and add in your vanilla extract and your peanut butter and stir constantly until your mixture is completely smooth. Once smooth, spoon over your crust and spread it using a silicone spatula. Set it aside to cool.

7. Now, as your filling cools, it's time to make the topping. Begin by adding your Stevia, butter, and chocolate to a clean pot and heating it to melting on low heat. Stir while heating to mix your ingredients.

8. Once all the ingredients are melted, add your cocoa powder and stir until your mixture is smooth again. Then add your Stevia and vanilla extract. Stir the

mixture once more to ensure it is completely smooth and spoon it over your shortbread and filling. Use your spatula again to smooth the chocolate topping out.

9. Set your baking dish aside to come to room temperature. Once it has cooled completely, cut it in to 16 pieces and serve!

Chapter Five: 6 Ketogenic Ice Cream Recipes

In this chapter, you will learn how to make the following sweet ketogenic ice cream recipes:

- Holiday Ice Cream

- Thanksgiving Pumpkin Ice Cream

- Ketogenic Strawberry Ice Cream

- Salty Butterscotch Ice Cream

- Peanut Butter Chocolate Ice Cream

- Ketogenic Coffee Ice Cream

- ## *Holiday Ice Cream*

Servings:	8
Nutrition Per Serving	
Calories:	131
Fat:	12g
Protein:	0g
Carbs:	3g
Sugar:	2g
Fiber:	0g

Ingredients

- 1-pint heavy cream

- 2 tbsp. dark chocolate chips

- 1.8 oz. shredded unsweetened coconut

- 1.8 oz. chopped strawberries

- 2 tbsp. Stevia

Directions:

1. Begin by adding your stevia and cream to a medium mixing bowl and whisking them together to get a consistent mixture.

2. Using a silicone spatula, now fold in your dark chocolate chips, strawberries, and coconut.

3. Once well combined, pour your ingredients in to bowl and cover. Put the bowl in the freezer and let it freeze overnight.

4. When ready to eat, sit your bowl in some warm water for just a few minutes to loosen up your ice cream from the bowl and then serve.

• *Thanksgiving Pumpkin Ice Cream*

*Note, this recipe requires an ice cream machine!

Servings:	4	
Nutrition Per Serving		
Calories:	369	
Fat:	34g	
Protein:	9g	
Carbs:	16g	
Sugar:	3g	
Fiber:	10g	

Ingredients

- ½ cup cottage cheese

- 2 tbsp. salted butter

- 2 cups coconut milk

- ½ cup chopped toasted pecans

- 2 egg yolks

- ½ cup pumpkin puree

- 1 tsp. maple extract

- 1 tsp. pumpkin spice

- ½ tsp. xanthan gum

- 20 drops liquid Stevia

- 1/3 cup erythritol

Directions:

1. In a small saucepan, combine your chopped pecans with your butter and heat on low.

2. While your butter melts, add your other ingredients in to a large mixing bowl and use your hand blender to blend them together thoroughly.

3. Once blended, pour your mixed ingredients in to your ice cream machine. Pour in your melted butter and pecan mixture after your other ingredients.

4. Follow the instructions for your ice cream machine to make ice cream.

- # *Ketogenic Strawberry Ice Cream*

Servings:	6
Nutrition Per Serving	
Calories:	174
Fat:	17g
Protein:	2.3g
Carbs:	16.6g
Sugar:	1.5g
Fiber:	0.6g

Ingredients

- 1 cup heavy cream

- 3 egg yolks

- 1 cup pureed strawberries

- 1/3 cup erythritol

- ½ tsp. vanilla extract

Directions:

1. Add your heavy cream to a small pot over low heat and stir while adding 1/3 cup of erythritol. Make sure that your cream doesn't boil, allow it to simmer only until your erythritol is dissolved.

2. Now, separate your whites from your yolks and put your yolks in to a medium sized mixing bowl. Beat the eggs with your hand mixer until they are twice the size and add in just a little of your hot cream mix while continuing to beat. Keep adding the cream a little at a time until your egg yolk mix has come to the same temperature as your cream. Then add in the rest of your cream while still beating the mixture with your hand mixer.

3. Next, add your vanilla extract and mix again to incorporate.

4. With your vanilla extract incorporated, chill your ingredients in the freezer for a couple of hours.

5. Once your mixtures are chilled, add your pureed strawberries to your chilled ingredients and mix slightly.

6. Chill your strawberry ice cream in the freezer overnight and then serve!

• *Salty Butterscotch Ice Cream*

*Note, this recipe requires an ice cream maker

Servings:	3
Nutrition Per Serving	
Calories:	228.6
Fat:	20.7g
Protein:	0.9g
Carbs:	11.4g
Sugar:	2g
Fiber:	0.4g

Ingredients

- 1 cup coconut milk

- 3 tbsp. butter

- 1 tsp. sea salt

- ¼ cup heavy cream

- ¼ cup sour cream

- 25 drops liquid sweetener

- 2 tbsp. vodka

- 2 tbsp. erythritol

- 2 tsp. butterscotch flavor / extract

- ½ tsp. xanthan gum

Directions:

1. In a large mixing bowl, combine your vodka, sour cream, butterscotch flavoring, coconut milk, heavy cream, salt, sweetener, and xanthan gum. Use your immersion blender to mix together well.

2. Now, add your butter to a saucepan and on low heat, brown it until caramel color.

3. Once your butter is browned, add it to your blended ingredients and blend it again.

4. Add your thoroughly blended mixture to your ice cream machine and follow the instructions for your ice cream machine to make your ice cream!

- ***Peanut Butter Chocolate Ice Cream***

Servings:	2
Nutrition Per Serving	
Calories:	362.6
Fat:	21.6g
Protein:	29.4g
Carbs:	14.4g
Sugar:	2.3g
Fiber:	3.5g

Ingredients

- 1 cup cottage cheese

- 2 tbsp. heavy cream

- 1 scoop protein powder (chocolate is best)

- 2 tbsp. natural smooth peanut butter

- 6 drops liquid sweetener

Directions:

1. In a large mixing bowl, combine your sweetener with your heavy cream, peanut butter and cottage cheese. Using an immersion blender, mix together all of your ingredients until you get a smooth consistency.

2. Once well mixed, add in your protein powder and mix again until your powder is incorporated.

3. Separate your mixture between two bowls and freeze for an hour before serving.

- ### *Ketogenic Coffee Ice Cream*

*Note, you will need an ice cream maker to make this recipe

Servings:	6
Nutrition Per Serving	
Calories:	314.7
Fat:	32.6g
Protein:	3.5g
Carbs:	4.1g
Sugar:	0.2g
Fiber:	0.2g

Ingredients

- ¼ cup coffee beans

- 1/8 tsp. salt

- 4 egg yolks

- 2 cups heavy whipping cream

- ½ cup unsweetened almond milk

- ¼ cup Splenda

- ½ tsp. vanilla extract

- ¼ tsp. xanthan gum

Directions:

1. In a large mixing bowl, combine your heavy cream, coffee beans, and almond milk and allow them to sit aside for 2 hours to infuse your coffee flavor.

2. After 2 hours, heat your mix of ingredients for 2 minutes in the microwave. After heating, strain your coffee beans out of the mixture.

3. Take your mixture without the beans and add in your vanilla, xanthan gum, Splenda, salt, and egg yolks. Stir thoroughly to combine your ingredients.

4. Microwave your mixture for 30 seconds and then stir. Microwave for another 30 seconds and stir again. Microwave once more for 30 more seconds and stir.

5. You now have a thick mixture. Strain the mixture through a sieve to eliminate any clumps.

6. Now, put your mix in to a bowl, cover, and put in the freezer for 30 minutes until chilled.

7. Once chilled, put your ice cream mix through your ice cream maker following the instructions of the manufacturer to make ice cream.

Chapter Six: 10 Other Ketogenic Dessert Recipes

In this chapter, you will learn how to make the following unique ketogenic dessert recipes:

- Ketogenic Maple Nut Muffins

- Ketogenic Lemon Scones

- Ketogenic Pumpkin Donut Holes

- Ketogenic Pink Lemonade Mousse

- Ketogenic Peanut Butter Chocolate Fudge

- Ketogenic Peanut Almond Butter Balls

- Ketogenic Raspberry Popsicles

- Ketogenic Peanut Butter Bombs

- Ketogenic Coconut Yogurt

- Chocolate Covered Bacon

- ## *Ketogenic Maple Nut Muffins*

Servings:	11
Nutrition Per Serving	
Calories:	245.7
Fat:	23.6g
Protein:	5.4g
Carbs:	10.1g
Sugar:	0.8g
Fiber:	8.1g

Ingredients

- 1 cup almond flour

- ½ tsp. baking soda

- 2 eggs

- ¾ cup pecan halves

- ½ cup golden flaxseed

- ½ tsp. apple cider vinegar

- ½ cup coconut oil

- ¼ cup erythritol

- ¼ tsp liquid Stevia

- 1 tsp. vanilla extract

- 2 tsp. maple extract

Directions:

1. Preheat your oven to 325 degrees. While your oven preheats, put paper muffin liners in to 11 holes in your muffin pan.

2. Now, add your pecan halves to your food processor and chop them until you get a coarse grind.

3. Now, take a large mixing bowl and combine your coconut oil, vanilla extract, liquid Stevia, eggs, maple extract, and apple cider vinegar. Use your hand mixer to mix these ingredients together thoroughly.

4. Take a clean mixing bowl, and 2/3 of your pecan halves, flaxseed, almond flour, baking soda, and erythritol. Use a silicone spatula to stir these ingredients together well.

5. Now, add your wet ingredients in to your dry ingredients and use your hand mixer to combine them completely.

6. Divide your batter between your cupcake liners and then sprinkle the rest of your pecans on top of the batter in each muffin cup.

7. Bake your muffins for 25 minutes or until cooked through.

Ketogenic Lemon Scones

Servings:	12
Nutrition Per Serving	
Calories:	130.8
Fat:	11.6g
Protein:	3.9g
Carbs:	4.7g
Sugar:	0.5g
Fiber:	2.1g

Ingredients

- 1 ½ cups almond flour

- ½ tsp. baking soda

- Dash of salt

- 1 egg

- 2 tbsp. coconut flour

- 3 ½ tbsp. room temperature butter

- 1 tbsp. whipping cream

- 1 tbsp. Stevia

- 1 tbsp. fresh lemon juice

- Zest of 1 lemon

Directions:

1. Preheat your oven to 350 degrees. While your oven preheats, cover a large baking tray with parchment paper.

2. In a medium mixing bowl, combine your Stevia and your room temperature butter. Cream together using your hand mixer until you get a light textured mixture.

3. Add the egg in to your mixing bowl and continue to mix. Once mixed well, add the rest of your ingredients and mix again to combine thoroughly.

4. Now, set your bowl aside for a few minutes while you tear off two sheets of parchment paper.

5. Stir the dough in your bowl and then dump it out on to a sheet of your parchment paper. Put the second sheet of parchment paper on top of the dough and use a rolling pin to roll out your dough to around ¾" thick.

6. Now, using a round cookie cutter to cut out 12 rounds from your dough. Set the rounds on your parchment covered baking sheet.

7. Bake your scones for 12 minutes or a little longer until cooked through.

- ## *Ketogenic Pumpkin Donut Holes*

Servings:	12
Nutrition Per Serving	
Calories:	112.3
Fat:	7.7g
Protein:	3.4g
Carbs:	9.4g
Sugar:	1.4g
Fiber:	4.2g

Ingredients

- ½ cup coconut flour

- ¼ tsp. salt

- 1 cup organic pumpkin puree

- 1/3 cup melted butter

- 3 eggs

- 2 tbsp. erythritol

- ¾ tsp. liquid Stevia

- 1 tsp. cardamom

- ¼ tsp. vanilla extract

- ¼ tsp. orange extract

Directions:

1. Preheat your oven to 325 degrees. While your oven is preheating, grease your muffin pan.

2. In a medium sized mixing bowl, combine your butter with the rest of your wet ingredients and stir thoroughly to mix well.

3. In a second mixing bowl, combine together your dry ingredients and stir thoroughly.

4. Now, use a sieve to sieve your dry ingredients in to your wet ingredients and then stir the resulting mixture.

5. Once all of your ingredients are well mixed, break your dough in to 12 pieces and roll each piece in to a small ball. Put each ball of dough in to one cupcake cup of your cupcake pan.

6. Bake your donut holes for 20 minutes or until golden brown.

- ***Ketogenic Pink Lemonade Mousse***

Servings:	6
Nutrition Per Serving	
Calories:	191
Fat:	16.4g
Protein:	4.2g
Carbs:	7.3g
Sugar:	4.4g
Fiber:	0g

Ingredients

- 8 oz. softened cream cheese

- 1 cup full fat milk

- 8 oz. thawed full fat whipped topping

- 1 ½ tsp. pink lemonade Crystal Light drink mix

Directions:

1. In a medium sized mixing bowl, combine your cream cheese with 1 ½ tsp. of your Crystal Light mix. Use your hand mixer to combine these ingredients thoroughly until smooth.

2. Continue mixing your ingredients while adding in your milk. Once blended, add in your whipped topping a little bit at a time while still blending.

3. Once well mixed, put your mousse in to a bowl and refrigerate for 3 hours or more until chilled.

• *Ketogenic Peanut Butter Chocolate Fudge*

Servings:	15
Nutrition Per Serving	
Calories:	177.5
Fat:	16.4g
Protein:	5.7g
Carbs:	17.6g
Sugar:	2g
Fiber:	3.6g

Ingredients

- 1 cup creamy natural peanut butter

- 8 oz. baking chocolate

- 1 cup Stevia

- ¾ cup erythritol

- ½ tsp. vanilla extract

- Dash of salt

Directions:

1. Using a double boiler, melt your chocolate slowly.

2. Once melted, add your chocolate in to a medium mixing bowl, and stir in the rest of your ingredients. Mix your ingredients thoroughly.

3. Taste your batter and see if you need to add a little more Stevia to sweeten.

4. If your batter is to your taste, pour it in to a loaf pan. Allow the fudge to come to room temperature and then refrigerate until chilled.

5. Once chilled, cut your fudge in to 15 pieces.

- ### *Ketogenic Peanut Almond Butter Balls*

Servings:	4
Nutrition Per Serving	
Calories:	173.3
Fat:	17g
Protein:	3.2g
Carbs:	4.9g
Sugar:	1.1g
Fiber:	1.3g

Ingredients

- 2 tbsp. natural creamy peanut butter

- 2 tbsp. heavy cream

- 2 tbsp. butter

- 2 tbsp. almond butter

- 4 drops liquid Stevia

- 1 ½ tsp. erythritol

Directions:

1. In a small bowl combine your almond butter, erythritol, heavy cream, butter, Stevia and peanut butter. Stir thoroughly to combine well.

2. Put your bowl of mixed ingredients in to the freezer and allow them to freeze for around 30 minutes until they firm up.

3. Once your ingredients have firmed up, roll your mixture in to four balls and serve!

- ***Ketogenic Raspberry Popsicles***

*Note, this recipe requires six popsicle molds

Servings:	6
Nutrition Per Serving	
Calories:	156.4
Fat:	15.7g
Protein:	0.8g
Carbs:	4.3g
Sugar:	1.1g
Fiber:	1.3g

Ingredients

- ¼ cup heavy cream

- 3.53 oz. raspberries

- ¼ cup sour cream

- 1 cup coconut milk

- ¼ cup coconut oil

- Juice of ½ lemon

- ½ tsp. guar gum

- 20 drops liquid stevia

Directions:

1. Add all of your ingredients in to a large mixing bowl and use your immersion blender to blend them together thoroughly.

2. Once blended well, put your mixture through a sieve to strain out any lumps or seeds.

3. Pour your strained mixture in to your popsicle molds and freeze for at least 3 hours to allow them to set before eating.

- ## *Ketogenic Peanut Butter Bombs*

Servings:	8
Nutrition Per Serving	
Calories:	211
Fat:	20.7g
Protein:	4.5g
Carbs:	4g
Sugar:	1g
Fiber:	2.5g

Ingredients

- ¼ cup cocoa powder

- 2 tbsp. heavy cream

- ¼ cup unsweetened shredded coconut

- 4 tbsp. peanut butter Fit Powder

- ½ cup coconut oil

- 6 tbsp. shelled hemp seeds

- 1 tsp. vanilla extract

- 28 drops liquid Stevia

Directions:

1. Cover a cookie sheet with parchment paper.

2. In a medium mixing bowl, combine your coconut oil with all of your dry ingredients. Mix them all together thoroughly with a silicone spatula until they are blended.

3. Add your vanilla, cream, and Stevia in to your ingredients and stir to mix together thoroughly again.

4. Pour out your coconut on to a plate.

5. Split your ingredient mix in to 8 pieces and roll each piece in to a ball. Roll each ball on your plate of coconut to cover it before setting on your cookie tray.

6. Put your cookie tray in to the freezer and let your peanut butter bombs firm up for 20 minutes before eating.

- ## *Ketogenic Coconut Yogurt*

Servings:	4
Nutrition Per Serving	
Calories:	317.1
Fat:	32.7g
Protein:	2.1g
Carbs:	5.3g
Sugar:	1.3g
Fiber:	0.3g

Ingredients

- 1 can full fat coconut milk

- 2/3 cup heavy whipping cream

- ½ tsp. xanthan gum

- 2 capsules probiotic-10

Directions:

1. Open up your can of coconut milk and stir it thoroughly to combine the milk and cream.

2. Divide your coconut milk between two mason jars with lids.

3. Break open one probiotic capsule in to each mason jar and stir the milk to disperse the probiotics.

4. Put the lid on your jars and then put the jars lid down on to a baking sheet in the oven and turn on the oven light. Leave the yogurt jars to sit for at least 12 hours.

5. After 12 hours, pour out your yogurt in to a mixing bowl and add in your xanthan gum. Now, use your hand mixer to thoroughly combine the gum and yogurt.

6. In a clean bowl, mix your heavy cream with your hand mixer until you see peaks forming. Once your peaks are stiff, mix the cream in to your yogurt mixture with your hand mixer.

7. Spoon your yogurt back in to your lidded mason jars and refrigerate to chill.

8. When you're ready to eat, serve your chilled yogurt with your choice of fresh fruit.

- ***Chocolate Covered Bacon***

Servings:	13 Slices
Nutrition Per Slice	
Calories:	95
Fat:	7.8g
Protein:	3.5g
Carbs:	5.9g
Sugar:	0.1g
Fiber:	0.5g

Ingredients

- 13 bacon slices

- 1 tbsp. maple extract

- 2 tbsp. erythritol

- ¼ cup roasted pecans chopped

- 2 tbsp. erythritol

- 4 tbsp. unsweetened cocoa powder

- 15 drops liquid Stevia

Directions:

1. Preheat your oven to 400 degrees. While your oven preheats, cover a large baking sheet with aluminum foil.

2. Spread your bacon slices out on to your baking sheet and sprinkle 2 tbsp. erythritol and maple extract over both sides of the bacon.

3. When your oven is preheated, bake your bacon for 45 minutes until it crisps. Then, remove the bacon from the oven and set it aside on a paper towel covered plate to cool.

4. Cover a new baking tray with parchment paper.

5. While your bacon cools, pour your bacon fat in to a large sized bowl and add in your liquid stevia, cocoa powder and 2 tbsp. erythritol. Mix these ingredients together well until fully mixed.

6. Now, dip your bacon slices in to your cocoa mixture so that they are completely covered. Once covered, spread your bacon out on your parchment paper covered tray and sprinkle your pecans over the bacon so that it sticks to your chocolate.

7. Put your bacon in to the refrigerator to chill for at least 6 hours before serving.

Tips to Help When Keto Cooking

When baking and cooking on the keto diet, or any diet for that matter, it can get a little flustering trying to keep up with nutrition. Below are some tips that can help you to organize and keep up with your keto cooking and baking process. I encourage you to implement these tips when trying the recipes in the chapters below.

- Keep a list of "forbidden" basic ingredients and foods as well as "permitted" ingredients and foods for quick reference. Make sure to make these lists identifiable from each other, however, by making them different colors or otherwise coding them.

- Have basic kitchen tools on hand such as measuring cups, measuring spoons, measuring jugs, parchment paper, and aluminum foil.

- Have storage containers on hand. Most of the keto recipes that you will come across will be for larger servings. In order to avoid eating more than one serving and to keep your food fresh make use of airtight containers and freezer safe containers.

- Write down basic nutrition information on the storage container of your stored items so that you don't have to dig up this information later.

- Don't be afraid to scale down recipes to make less of something if you are single or just have a small family. Just be sure to accurately scale down everything in your recipe as well, or better yet, make the full batch and share with friends!

- Find substitutions. If you are running low on something or find a recipe you love that isn't keto friendly, hop online and research keto friendly ingredient substitutions! Don't worry though, the recipes in this book are all keto friendly!

Conclusion

I hope that by trying your hand at the recipes in the chapters above, you will not only find satisfaction for your sweet tooth, but that you will also learn how to put together your own keto friendly sweets! By following the ingredient lists and instructions for the recipes that I have shared, you can quickly and easily combine your favorites to come up with something new. Just remember to keep it simple, keep it affordable, and keep it keto!

Made in the USA
San Bernardino, CA
08 December 2016